Learn To Successfully Navigate The Medicare Maze!

Discover Medicare Rules, Enrollment Periods and Penalties with 15 Successful Tried & True Facts & Tools

Did you know that in the United States 9,000 people a day are turning 65!

In this informative Itty Bitty Book, Joyce Khoury shows you how to navigate through this complicated journey, carefully and methodically so as to understand the best choices for you and the future of your health.

Use these important 15 tools and tips so you can develop a safe way to protect yourself through life's unexpected medical adventures.

For example:

- Understand why you need to have Part B as soon as you are eligible.
- Learn about the differences between all the plans available and how they can benefit you the most.
- Understand the basis for Medicare and why it is a gift to us as aging Americans.

Pick up a copy of this powerful book today and experience confidence in knowing how to navigate through this Medicare Maze!

Your Amazing Itty Bitty® Medicare Book:

15 Key Steps to Successfully Navigate Medicare.

Joyce Khoury

Published by Itty Bitty® Publishing
A subsidiary of S & P Productions, Inc.

Copyright © 2016 Joyce Khoury

Printed in the United States of America

Itty Bitty Publishing
311 Main Street, Suite D
El Segundo, CA 90245
(310) 640-8885

ISBN: 978-0-9992211-1-2

Dedication

Thank you to my mother and father for helping me understand that every person we encounter in our life matters.

Thank you to my entire family for the amazing, unconditional support I receive from them every single day no matter what my dreams.

And....thank you to the universe for showing me there is always going to be way to help our fellow human beings no matter what the issue is.

Stop by our Itty Bitty® website to find to interesting blog entries regarding ……….

www.IttyBittyPublishing.com

Or visit Joyce at

www.medicarecoach101.com

Table of Contents

Introduction

Today is your lucky day! You are now eligible to receive Medicare!

Medicare is truly a gift, considering the complicated and expensive health insurance environment we are currently living in.

For most people, choosing a Medicare Plan can be intimidating, especially since it is usually the first time you have ever made these choices without the help of an employer.

Let the 15 Chapters in this book set up a roadmap to navigate the Medicare Maze so that you can rest assured you are on the right path.

Step 1
When Should You Start
Thinking About Medicare?

Medicare came into existence in 1965 and was made law by President Lyndon Baynes Johnson. It was insurance for those aged 65. This was the age when most people retired and no longer had the option of being covered by their employer's insurance.

1. Today, most people are still employed at age 65 so the best time to start thinking about Medicare insurance is around your 64th birthday. Employed or not, you become eligible for Medicare at age 65 and you will have to decide which plan is best for you.

2. Explore your options. Find someone you can trust who is knowledgeable about the subject of Medicare. You may be eligible to keep your employer's group insurance coverage instead of opting to use your Medicare eligibility. Find out how this choice may affect you and your family.

Who Should You Talk To About Your Medicare Choices?

If you are employed

- This can be your HR/Benefits manager,
- A doctor or,
- Best of all, your local Medicare insurance specialist.

If you are self-employed or not employed

- The best choice for advice is your local Medicare specialist.

Step 2
Medicare When You Are 65 and Gainfully Employed

There is some confusion about when to utilize your Medicare eligibility when you are still employed. Here are a few points to consider.

1. Ask your HR/Benefits manager if your employer will allow you to continue using group health insurance coverage for you and your family. If not, ask if they offer a retiree insurance plan. Find out how much it will cost and whether it is a PPO plan or an HMO plan.
2. Ask for a provider list to see if your doctor is part of the network for that type of insurance.
3. Find out what type of prescription drug coverage your employer can offer, if there is a deductible and what the co-pays are. Find out what is the cost of the drugs you are currently taking.
4. Ask your employer if the coverage includes Dental, Vision and Hearing.
5. If you work for the city or state, you will have a different type of insurance coverage and may not even need Medicare.

Important Questions

- Does your company have a HR/Benefits Manager?
- Does your employer offer group or retiree health insurance to you?
- Does that coverage include prescription drug coverage?
- What about coverage for your family if they are not eligible yet for Medicare?
- Does your employer coverage include coverage for dental, vision and/or hearing?
- Did you contribute to the FICA tax system for a minimum of 10 years or 40 quarters?

Step 3
Medicare When You Are 65 And No Longer Employed

If you turn 65 and decide to retire, you will be faced with making your own Medicare Plan choices. This is when you should seek professional advice from people who are familiar with the Medicare Maze.
To do this you can:

1. Contact Medicare or Social Security directly; contact an independent Medicare Insurance Specialist; or, ask your doctor if he or she can recommend someone to talk to.
2. If you are married perhaps your spouse is covered by his/her employer's group insurance and you can be added to that plan.
3. Be aware that in order to be eligible to receive Medicare Part A at no charge, you must have worked for a minimum of ten years (40 quarters) and contributed to FICA, Federal Insurance Contributions Act tax.
4. If you are on a fixed-income and worried about future medical costs, you will need to understand what the different Medicare Plans can offer.

Tips To Keep In Mind

- Be sure to seek out professional advice. Independent insurance agents are a great source of information and they are available to you at no charge.
- Investigate the possibility of being covered on your spouse's insurance plan.
- Confirm you have worked the required number of quarters/years for Medicare Part A to be no cost. You can also be eligible for Medicare Part A if you did not work but your spouse worked depending on your current marital status.
- Depending on your income requirements, learn how the different Medicare Plans work so you can make the best decision for your health needs.

Step 4
Medicare When You Are On Disability

This particular subject can be extremely tricky and it may require you to contact an attorney to help you understand your rights. First and foremost know that Workmen's Compensation Disability Coverage is not health coverage in total. It is only coverage for the particular disability you have incurred.

1. Once you are on Workmen's Compensation Disability Insurance, know that it is not permanent and it is insurance that covers only the disability matter. You need to confirm whether you will be keeping or losing your employer's group health plan.
2. Depending on your disability, you may be eligible to receive social security disability benefits.
3. Once you have been receiving social security disability benefits for 24 months, you will then be eligible for Medicare even if you are under 65.

Important Tips For Medicare When You Are On Disability

- Determine what level of disability you are on, whether it is permanent or temporary
- Determine whether you will still be covered by your employer's group plan
- Consult a social security disability insurance attorney to be sure that you will have enough credits for Part A to be eligible to receive Part A of Medicare at no cost when you become eligible.

Step 5
Medicare And Citizenship

In order to be eligible to receive Medicare benefits you must be a legal resident living in the United States for a minimum of 5 years.

1. If you have a green card, eligibility for Medicare is determined 5 years from the date you received your green card.
2. If you have worked a number of years overseas, yet still contributed to FICA, you may still be eligible to receive Medicare.
3. You must have worked the minimum requirement of 10 years or 40 quarters and contributed to FICA (Federal Insurance Contributions Act tax) in order to be eligible to receive Part A at no cost.
4. You must have documentation from your employer overseas in order to determine eligibility for Part A.

Tips For Medicare Eligibility If You Are An Immigrant Or Naturalized Citizen

- Eligibility is granted 5 years from the date of receiving your green card
- If you worked overseas and as long as the required number of credits have been earned, you will be eligible to have Part A at no cost.
- Keep in mind that you may have to consult with an immigration attorney to determine how to get Part A FICA credits.

Step 6
Permanent Penalties In Medicare

If you do not sign up for Medicare Part B or D (prescription drug coverage) within specified time limits, you will incur a ***permanent*** penalty.

1. The Part B penalty is calculated as 1% /month of the premium for Part B in that specific year. The penalty can increase as the premium for Part B also increases.
2. The Part B penalty amounts to an extra 10 percent for every full 12 month period that has elapsed between your Initial Enrollment Period and the time you finally sign up.
3. The Part D penalty is calculated as 1%/month of the average premium for a prescription drug plan for that year. This penalty can also increase or decrease due to the changing premiums for prescription drug plans each year.

Permanent Penalties In Medicare

- There are specific time limits attached to penalties both for Part B and Part D
- The penalty for Part B is 1%/month of the premium calculated for that specific year or 10% over a 12 month period.
- The penalty for Part D is 1%/month of the national average premium (*NAP*) per year or 12% a year.
- Both Part B and Part D penalties can change due to the changes in Part D premiums as well as cost of Part B.

Step 7
Is Part A Of Medicare
Always $0 Cost?

Medicare is composed of Part A (Hospitalization and Skilled Nursing facility) and Part B (all doctor's services including x-rays, screenings, etc.) In order to earn Medicare Part A at no cost when you become eligible, you must have worked a minimum of 10 years or 40 quarters.

Requirements for premium-free Part A:

1. You must have worked a minimum of 40 quarters or 10 years and paid into FICA (Federal Insurance Contributions Act tax) in order to earn Part A of Medicare at no charge.
2. For non-citizens, you must have **both** a green card **and** legal residency for 5 years and you must have worked a minimum of 40 quarters or 10 years and paid into the FICA tax system in order for Part A to be $0 cost.
3. If you worked less than the 30 quarters Part A will cost $422; if you worked 30-39 quarters Part A will cost $232.

Part A of Medicare Is Not Always $0 Cost

- If you paid Medicare taxes for less than 30 quarters, the standard Part A premium is $422.00
- If you paid Medicare taxes for 30-39 quarters, the standard Part A premium is $232.00

Step 8
Applying For Part B

There are certain guidelines for applying for Part B when you become eligible to enroll in Medicare. It does not always happen automatically. If you do not apply within the specified timelines as outlined in a previous chapter, you will incur penalties.

1. If you are already receiving social security benefits prior to turning 65, when you become 65 you are automatically enrolled in Part B.
2. If you are employed and not receiving social security benefits, your HR/Benefits should explain to you how to enroll into Part B.
3. If you are not employed, turning 65 and not receiving social security benefits yet, you need to apply for Part B either online, at the social security office or get help from a Medicare insurance specialist.
4. If you do not apply within the specified time limit, you will have a penalty added on to your Part B premium which increases as time goes by.

Applying For Part B

- You will be automatically enrolled in Part B if you are already receiving social security benefits.
- You will need to sign up for Part B if you are not employed and/or not receiving social security benefits.
- You must be aware of the timelines for enrolling into Part B so you can avoid incurring a penalty.

Step 9
Applying For Part D

It is a requirement that you sign up for a Prescription Drug Plan (Part D) when you become eligible for Medicare. You have 63 days to sign up after your 65th birthday. If you wait until after that time, a penalty will be assessed for the amount of months in which you had no prescription drug coverage.

1. The best way to choose a prescription drug plan is to make sure any medications you are taking currently are on the formulary in the plan you choose. If your drug is not on the formulary, then it will not be covered.
2. The monthly premium of prescription drug plans vary greatly. Some plans have a deductible, some do not. The price of a drug on one plan may differ greatly from the price of the same drug on another plan.
3. Prescription drugs have different co-pays and are priced on a tiered system.
4. If you take a large amount of prescription drugs, you may reach what is known as the "Donut Hole" and you will have to pay a higher co-pay for your medication.

Things You Should Know About Drug Costs

- Tier 1 through Tier 5.
  - Tier 1 and 2 are usually generic and lower in cost.
  - Tier 3 and Tier 4 are Brand name drugs and
  - Tier 5 is a specialty drug and is much more expensive.
- You can save money if you buy your prescription drugs from what is known as a "preferred pharmacy" and/or if you buy a 90-day supply through mail order.
- You can find preferred pharmacies in the directories for each prescription drug plan and save money on your medications

Step 10
What About Dental Coverage?

Many people do not realize that dental coverage is not always part of basic medical coverage. It is usually a stand-alone plan with limitations and co-pays.

1. Original Medicare does not provide dental coverage.
2. Check your medical plan carefully if you wish to have dental coverage. Dental coverage is an ancillary service and not necessarily part of your medical plan. Not all plans incorporate dental coverage. Some HMO Plans offer dental coverage but not all. Medicare Supplement Plans do not include dental coverage.
3. If you have a dental plan, be sure you understand how it works. There is usually a premium, a waiting period, co-pays and limitations on coverage. Each dental service is coded by the American Dental Ass. (ADA) and is priced accordingly. Be sure and get an estimate from your dentist before you agree to the procedure.
4. Some dental plans have a 6-12 month waiting period before you are covered for comprehensive services such as crowns, root canals and bridges.

Tips About Dental Coverage

- Dental coverage is usually separate from your basic medical plan.
- Medicare does not cover dental plans
- Dental plans have many parts. Be sure to know the co-pays, specific coverages and services.
- Get an estimate for all dental work before agreeing to the procedure.
- Confirm that your dentist is in the network.
- Confirm whether or not the service is preventive or comprehensive so you can understand the charges.

Step 11
What About Vision Coverage?

Unlike dental care, many HMO Plans do cover vision care, but it is important to find out what your plan does cover before you need it.

1. Original Medicare does not provide vision coverage.
2. Most Medicare HMO plans include coverage for vision care. Typically you get one eye exam per year at a designated vision care facility. Glasses and contacts are discounted and the discount varies from plan to plan.
3. Medicare Supplement Plans do not include vision coverage for glasses or contacts.
4. Be aware of the difference between your Ophthalmologist and your Optometrist. Ophthalmologist is for the general health of your eyes, such as cataracts, macular degeneration, etc. Optometrist is for glasses and contacts.

Vision Coverage

- Vision coverage is not part of Medicare.
- HMO plans usually incorporate vision care.
- Medicare Supplement plans do not support vision plans.
- Vision plans cover eye examinations, glasses and contacts.
- Cataract surgery is covered by your ophthalmologist and your Medicare plan.

Step 12
Coverage For Hearing Aids

As you age, your hearing can diminish substantially. Therefore, hearing aids have become an important benefit to have in your Medicare Plan.

1. Medicare does not provide hearing aids.
2. Some Medicare Advantage Plans include coverage for hearing tests and hearing aids, but not all. If you need that benefit, be sure to check if your plan includes hearing aid coverage.
3. Some Medicare Advantage Plans offer the hearing benefit in the form of a discount instead of actual hearing aids.
4. Medicare Supplements do not include coverage hearing aids.

Coverage For Hearing Aids

- Hearing aids are not covered by Medicare.
- If your plan is a Medicare Advantage Plan, check to see if it offers hearing aid coverage.
- Medicare Supplement Plans do not offer coverage for hearing aids.

Step 13
Differences Between Original Medicare, Medicare Supplement Plans And Medicare Advantage Plans

1. Original Medicare is composed of Part A for Hospitalization and Part B for all other medical services such as X-rays, radiologic services, doctor visits and ambulance services. It does not provide coverage for ancillary services such as dental, vision and hearing.

2. Medicare Supplement Plans are sold through private insurance carriers and have a monthly premium based on the age of the consumer. They do not provide coverage for ancillary services such as dental, vision and hearing.

3. Medicare Advantage Plans function through a network of Medical Groups and are subsidized by the government. You must use a physician that is part of the network or medical group in order to be covered by the Plan. These plans do provide coverage for ancillary services such as dental, vision hearing and fitness memberships and much more.

Important Tips To Know About The Different Medicare Plans

- Original Medicare only pays up to 80 percent of your medical costs
- Medicare Supplement Plans have a monthly premium and the pricing is based on the age of the individual.
- Medicare Supplement Plans have up to 11 different choices with varying co-pays and deductibles.
- Most Medicare Advantage Plans in Los Angeles County have a $0 premium and almost always include a prescription drug plan.
- Medicare Advantage Plans include ancillary services such as dental, vision and hearing, fitness memberships, acupuncture and chiropractic services, transportation and a 24-hour nurse line.

Step 14
You Have A Right To Accurate Information

Although working through the Medicare process can be tedious and very confusing, you as the consumer are well protected against fraudulent or incompetent activity.

1. There are many different channels you can access if you feel you have been treated unfairly or incompetently.
2. One important point to remember is always be prepared with proof and notes of your conversations. This will allow Social Security or any other entity to investigate your grievance properly and fairly.

Ways To Obtain Accurate Information

Here are some ways you can address a problem
with Medicare that you feel must be addressed.
For contact information on each one of these
organizations please go:
www.medicarecoach101.com

Contact:

- Social Security administration
- Centers for Medicare & Medicaid
  Services
- State Health Insurance Assistance
  Program (SHIP)
- Requesting Equitable Relief through
  Social Security
- Contact a Medicare Ombudsman
- Contact your Quality Improvement
  Organization (QIO)
- Contact your Insurance Carrier
- Filing a grievance with your Medicare
  Plan
- Filing a Formal Appeal through Medicare

Step 15
Other Insurance Options In Conjunction With Medicare

There are a number of institutions that offer health insurance options. We can discuss some of them in this chapter.

1. Medicaid assistance is based on the federal poverty level. This type of assistance includes In-Home Support Services (IHSS), food programs, utilities services and discounts on medications.
2. PACE programs are Programs of All-Inclusive Care for the Elderly. PACE helps seniors with daily needs such as meals, transportation and counseling.
3. Employer-based insurance and Medicare work together based on the number of employees at the company. Please confirm whether your employer is Primary or Secondary to Medicare.
4. Medicare and Employer-Based Retiree Benefits can be complicated. Be aware of obtaining and paying for Part B so that your retiree coverage is "creditable".
5. COBRA is not creditable coverage. Do not accept COBRA insurance without paying for Part B. Otherwise, you will face penalties and delays in your Medicare coverage.

Other Options In Conjunction With Medicare

- Medicaid assistance (also known as Medi-Cal only in the state of California) is based on income.
- PACE programs are all inclusive and provide services for the frail and elderly.
- Employer-based coverage is either primary or secondary to Medicare depending on the number of employees in the company.
- COBRA insurance is expensive and is not creditable insurance.
- Always obtain and pay for Part B when you are eligible unless you are covered under your employer's group health plan. That way you will not incur a needless permanent penalty.

You've finished. Before you go...

Tweet/share that you finished this book.

Please star rate this book.

Reviews are solid gold to writers. Please take a few minutes to give us some itty bitty feedback.

ABOUT THE AUTHOR

Life is like a "Box of Chocolates" as Forrest Gump said, and for Joyce Khoury nothing could be closer to the truth!

Joyce was born in 1951. This was the beginning of a time of tremendous change in society, technology, economics, culture and much more. Until then, most people followed traditional ideas that were direct and expected. But starting in the 50's and beyond, so much of the world exploded into creative, innovative and truly ground-breaking pathways.

Born of humble, immigrant parents from Canada, Joyce grew up in New Bedford, Massachusetts and began to experience life to the fullest. She was the first person in her family to attend college. She married a man from half-way across the world, had four amazing daughters and always worked to support her family and herself as they progressed through their life journey.

Joyce's various job experiences helped her gain a tremendous understanding of how to help people and today she finds her career as a Medicare Insurance Specialist one of the most satisfying endeavors of her life. By helping each person make the choice of choosing their health care plan, Joyce has had the opportunity to meet people from all walks of life who continue to offer so much to society.

Each client has an important and interesting story to tell and Joyce feels it is a gift to have a career at this stage of her life that is so helpful and allows her to contribute to their understanding of living a healthier, happier life.

Joyce can be reached at:
www.medicarecoach.com

If you liked this Itty Bitty® book you might also enjoy...

- **Your Amazing Itty Bitty® Self-Esteem Book** – Jade Elizabeth

- **Your Amazing Itty Bitty® Heal Your Body Book** – Patricia Garza Pinto

- **Your Amazing Itty Bitty® Veterans Survival Book** – Earl J. Katigbak

Or any of our other Itty Bitty® books available on line.